The
Garfield
How To Party Book

The Garfield
How To Party Book

by Jim Davis

BALLANTINE BOOKS · NEW YORK

Library of Congress Catalog Card Number: 87-91553

ISBN: 0-345-35180-8 (party pack)

ISBN: 0-345-35724-8 (book)

Manufactured in the United States of America

First Edition: June 1988

10 9 8 7 6 5 4 3 2 1

555-3825 ✻✻✻

INTRODUCTION

Garfield and I share one very simple philosophy: "The only legitimate pursuit in life is happiness." Given this, it stands to reason that having fun makes us happier than not having fun. And the best way to have fun is to party!

This book presents a daring new concept in partying, namely, that parties can be held anytime, anywhere, for any reason. You don't need to have a noisemaker and a cake to have a party. All you need is motivation, opportunity, and a contempt for decorum.

The Garfield How to Party Book is basically an *alternative* party book. While some of the parties suggested here are variations on more traditional parties, others explore uncharted party vistas.

Parties lurk everywhere. There may be a party in your sock drawer, under your bed, in your lunch box, or by the photocopy machine. Parties are there for those with the imagination to conceive them and the courage to pursue them.

JIM DAVIS

Garfield's PARTY PLEDGE

I, _____,
do solemnly, yet with some giggling,
vow to preserve, protect, and propa-
gate the true spirit of partying by
celebrating wherever and whenever
possible; and to attain and uphold
my bad reputation as a party animal
through affronts to common decency
and otherwise fun behavior; which, if
I don't, may I spend the rest of my life
chained to someone who thinks
cockroaches are "really
interesting."

THE OFFICIAL SEAL OF GREAT FUN

PARTYING

through the

AGES

 brief yet completely unreliable survey of mankind's quest for the perfect party.

Prehistoric man found it very difficult to party, because no one had invented the weekend. When he did have a get-together, it was usually a "Come As You Have Evolved So Far" party.

The ancient Egyptians worshipped a party god known as "Rama-Lama." On the first day of each new year, Rama-Lama was honored with solemn religious rites, during which the pharaoh would crush a drinking goblet against his forehead, then sacrifice a rubber chicken.

The famous Greek philosopher Socrates would spend an entire party discussing concepts like "justice" and "term life insurance." Consequently, he was convicted of being a "party pooper," and was introduced to the party game "Drink Hemlock Until You Croak."

The Romans threw toga parties which were so wild, crude, and depraved that they could be found on any college campus today. The Romans also developed the food fight, the water balloon, and an early form of "Musical Chairs," in which the losers were fed to the lions.

The spirit of partying survived the Dark Ages, thanks to dedicated groups of Irish monks who patiently copied and re-copied jokes from old Roman cocktail napkins.

During the Middle Ages the most popular types of parties were the merchants fair, the jousting tournament, and the Hundred Years War. There was a slight drop-off in celebrating in the fourteenth century, when it was not unusual for parties to end early because all the guests had died of the Black Plague.

Ancient Chinese parties often featured fireworks. On one occasion a cherry bomb accidentally exploded in the hat of the great Chinese sage Confucius and for the next three years he told nothing but "Knock, Knock" jokes.

Good times returned to Europe during the Renaissance, as people rediscovered classics like the "Tupperware Party" and the "Shriners Convention." And Michelangelo painted the Sistine Chapel, just for fun.

The Puritans came to America seeking the freedom to party in their own way. Curiously enough, their idea of having a good time was to sit around not having one, while making sure no one else was having one either.

King Louis XVI and Marie Antoinette held many elegant and sumptuous balls at the magnificent palace of Versailles. This enraged the French peasants, who could not party because they were too poor to afford coasters. Revolution followed.

It is a little known fact that Napoleon lost the battle of Waterloo because he was busy throwing a polka party for his general staff. In his memoirs, Napoleon expressed regret at losing the battle, but insisted that he could still "polka the pants off any general in Europe."

In the days of the Wild West, fun was in such short supply that gangs of rustlers would often steal an entire party, including the paper plates and dip. "Charades" was always a popular party game, particularly if the two teams were allowed to exchange gunfire.

In 1912 a group of politicians headed by Teddy Roosevelt decided to organize a Bull Moose Party. However, as the moose refused to talk politics, trashed the buffet, and were generally very hard on the furniture, the idea was a flop.

People partied hearty during the "Roaring '20s." Gangsters like Al Capone often threw lavish "rubbing out" parties, where it was not unusual for the guest of honor to get into a conga line and disappear from the face of the earth.

The creation of rock and roll in the 1950s meant that parties could now be so much fun it would drive your neighbors up the wall. Young people went to "sock hops," at which there was actually very little hopping, which eventually led to Woodstock, where very few people even wore socks.

And they all had a really good time.

CHAPTER TWO

Party Etiquette

or never mind your manners

A concise guide to improper party behavior

• At a party, it is never considered proper to belch politely. Always try to achieve a belch that will register on the Richter Scale.

• When chugging the punchbowl, always remember to keep the pinky fingers extended, and try to slosh as much as possible into your shoes.

• Wearing a lamp shade before 10 p.m. is considered bad taste. Lamps, however, may be worn at any time, except in the pool or shower.

• At a dinner party, it is never considered polite to ask for a doggy bag. Always remember to bring your own.

• Crashing a party is acceptable behavior, provided that you aren't crashing it with your car. If you do crash a party with your car, don't forget to say "Excuse me" to anyone you may have run over.

• It is considered good party form to eat without using one's hands, and most veteran partygoers use the so-called "backhoe method." This involves throwing one's

face down into a bowl of food and gouging out great mouthfuls with the upper lip and teeth. Above all, never wipe your face on your sleeve; that's what drapes are for.

• Always bring something to a party. Preferably a flagrant disregard for common decency, and an empty stomach.

• When responding to an R.S.V.P., it is considered stiff and stodgy to make use of the telephone or the mails. Always reply via a large rock with note attached, or a flaming arrow.

• If your stay at a party extends beyond six months, you should kick in a few bucks for more potato chips.

• While dancing, always cling tightly to your partner, in case one of you starts to fall off the table.

• With regard to food, be sure to follow the proper sequence of courses. Appetizers should always be thrown first, followed by the salad course, main course, and the dessert course, of course.

17

CHAPTER THREE

Holiday PARTIES

OR-TRADITIONS WERE MADE TO BE BROKEN

When it comes to holiday celebrating, most people prefer traditional activities like Halloween muskrat racing or trimming the automatic garage-door opener at Christmas. In addition to these general customs, most families have their own special holiday traditions, all of them fraught with historical significance that no one remembers anymore. Still, there's always room for improvement! If you're growing bored with these time-honored rituals, here are some alternative ideas for holiday fun!

THE UNWANTED CHRISTMAS GIFT EXCHANGE

Start the new year with a party that helps clear away the debris from the old year! You know that fur spaghetti strainer you got from Aunt Gladys? That rhinestone tie from Cousin Ed? This is your chance to wrap them up and foist them on someone else! Have each guest bring a present that they're just dying to part with. Then place them all in a pile, decide on a "picking order," and have everyone make a selection. Who knows? You might get something weird enough to suit your taste!

While you're at it, why not make this an opportunity to clear out those holiday leftovers? Ask each guest to bring along some treat that managed to survive the holiday scarfing. If everyone brings fruitcake, well, you can always order pizza, and the fruitcakes are handy for cracking walnuts.

THE "CUP RUNNETH OVER" PARTY

Valentine's Day is a day for expressing our feelings for others, and here's a party where you get the chance to really lay it on thick! Prior to the party, each guest must select someone to be the object of their affections. It doesn't matter if it's a spouse, parent, sibling, boyfriend, girlfriend, friend friend, or even pet, as long as this person or thing is going to be present at the party. They must then conceive and rehearse a heartfelt tribute to the object of their affections. Then, on the night of the party, each guest must compete in a sort of "Devotion Derby," where the object is to perform the most moving, sincere, original, and/or outrageous tribute to your chosen person. How you express your devotion is entirely up to you. You might compose and recite a poem. You could sing your sentiments, or paint them, or mime them. You could sacrifice a favorite tennis shoe in your loved one's honor. If two people want to extol the same person, they could perform a duet. Give a prize for the best performance. Anyone who elicits tears from the object of their affections should automatically make the semi-finals.

Love is a mysterious and powerful emotion, so who knows what will come of your efforts. New relationships may blossom, old ones may wither. It's quite likely that romance will be set back 200 years. But it's bound to be an interesting evening!

THE ALL-GREEN GALA

It's St. Patrick's Day! Time to get green and party! Salute the auld sod with a party that's as green as you can get it. Serve naturally green foods like celery, peppers, pickles, green olives, guacamole, avocado dip, and lime sherbet. Then make sure you add plenty of *un*naturally green munchies. A little green food coloring will give eggs, milk, onions, mashed potatoes, cakes, and cook-ies the proper hue. Don't forget to decorate with plenty of green crepe paper. If you really plan ahead, you might even be able to feature several all-green strands of Christmas lights. For that extra added dimension of greenness, consider holding this party in a greenhouse, a pool hall, or on a golf course—assuming there's enough green in your wallet to cover it.

THE EASTER BONNET BASH

Easter bonnets are traditionally adorned with things like ribbons and flowers. But wouldn't it be more fun to wear a bonnet decorated with something more interesting? Like a live chicken, perhaps. Throw a party where all the guests must wear Easter bonnets that they have fashioned themselves. Give a prize for the most outrageous design.

Whatever type of Easter bash you're hosting, you can raise the excitement level with a round of "Easter Egg Roulette." How to play: Color several dozen eggs, some raw, some hardboiled, and place them together in a pile. A player then selects an egg, without touching it. Will it be raw or hardboiled? You'll find out when a second person holds the egg above the player's head, then cracks it! (The egg will break a lot easier if you crack it on the edge of a counter first.) Any player unlucky enough to have selected a raw egg will wind up with egg on his face! Want to add an element of competition? Have two players go "head to head"! Break the eggs at the same time, and see who gets egged! Want to play this game at other times besides Easter? Go right ahead! Eggs are cheap!

THE "START YOUR OWN COUNTRY" PARTY

When the American colonists broke away from the English crown, they were suddenly faced with a lot of tough decisions, such as what to do with all their "God Save the King" sweatshirts and bumper stickers. Not to mention that they had to decide how to govern themselves. That wasn't such an easy task, as you will discover by throwing a "Start Your Own Country" party.

Assume that you and your guests are about to form a brand new, sovereign state. Here are some of the political options you'll have to discuss:

● What type of government will we have?

☐ democracy (government by the people)
☐ theocracy (government by the clergy)
☐ aristocracy (government by the upper classes)
☐ autocracy (government by General Motors)

● Who will be our new head of state?

☐ the strongest
☐ the smartest
☐ the wealthiest
☐ the loudest

(This might be the moment for a brief political campaign, complete with nominations, speeches, debates, and above all, scandal and mudslinging.)

● Who should be allowed to vote?

☐ everyone
☐ everyone above a certain age
☐ everyone of a certain sex
☐ everyone who is certain of their age and sex

Once you get some of these things ironed out, you'll need to pass some laws. Here's your chance to ram through that legislation you've always wanted to see enacted! Make double parking a capital offense! Institute the five-hour work week! Outlaw war, loansharking, and xylophone music! Make any law you like! It's your country!

And don't forget to decide on such other important issues as taxation, weights and measures, the postal system, monetary system, and who will represent your country at the next Olympic games. If you get tired of these domestic questions, think about starting a war with the party next door. By midnight you may have conquered your entire block!

THE
END OF SUMMER
WAKE

Labor day traditionally marks the end of the summer, so get the gang together to mourn the passing of another fun season. Put the last burgers of summer on the grill, take one last dip in the pool, and play a final game of volleyball. Have each of your guests make a list of the fun things he or she did that summer. Then pass out black armbands and have everyone gather around a fire in the grill. As the sun sets, each guest should toss his list of summer fun into the fire. For good measure you might want to add a pair of shorts, vacation brochures, or an old Beach Boys tape.

Then, once that solemn ceremony has concluded, crank up the stereo and have a great time—because no matter what time of year it is, it's always the party season!

THE "MYSTERY GUESTS" PARTY

Have you ever read Edgar Allan Poe's story "The Masque of the Red Death"? (You do read other things besides party books, right?) Anyway, in this story, a mysterious stranger comes to this prince's party, and everyone gets bent out of shape because the stranger turns out to be Death. Well, this party idea is a lot like that, except the mystery guest turns out to be "Chuck, from Accounting."

Here's the plot: You and your friends are invited to a Halloween costume party by a mutual friend. All of you accept the invitation. The host is delighted. Prior to the party, however, each of you enlists another person, someone unknown to the host, to attend the party in your place. On the night of the party you and your friends gather at a location near the host's place. Your "mystery guests" go the party. They wear costumes that completely conceal their features. They don't speak when the host addresses them. The host is surprised and disconcerted to be hosting a party full of silent strangers. Things get really spooky. Just when the host is on the verge of calling the police, one of the "mystery guests" calls you, instead. You and your friends descend upon the party, bearing armloads of extra refreshments (since the party is now a much larger party), and restoring your friend's sanity. Everyone has a good time, and your host has nightmares about this for years. End of party.

THE "THANKSGIVING 2400" PARTY

The Pilgrims and Indians celebrated the first Thanksgiving in 1621, nearly 400 years ago. They ate turkey and deer meat and argued about who should wash the dishes. Much of our traditional Thanksgiving cuisine dates from those early colonial times. And that's the problem! Here we are in a late-twentieth-century high-tech society, and we're still eating like we just got off Plymouth Rock! Let's look to the future of Thanksgiving! Say, 400 years or so into the future!

Imagine it's 2400 A.D. and the whole family is about to gather at your pod to chow down and watch robots play football on the laser scanner. What will you be eating? Ask your guests to bring dishes that approximate their idea of future food. Maybe it's chocolate-covered broccoli, or sardines on a stick or, for the more traditional, turkey stuffed with pasta. Dessert could be wiener pudding or ice cream topped with marshmallows and corn. Be creative! (But *do* make sure that everything to be eaten is indeed safe to eat.) Who knows? You may discover some new taste treats that are centuries ahead of their time!

THE "BUT WILL THIS DO?" GIFT EXCHANGE

Like it says in the old carol, "Tis the season to be greedy!" Or something like that. Here's a funny and inexpensive way to jolly up your office, school, or club gift-exchange. Sometime prior to the party, everyone participating should write his or her name on a slip of paper along with a description of the gift they would like more than anything in the world. The slips are then placed in a hat, and each person draws one, being sure not to draw his or her own, and keeping the name they have selected a secret. Then you go out and buy a gift that is a rough—sometimes *very* rough—approximation of the gift the recipient wished for. For example, if they wished for a Ferrari, buy them a toy Ferrari, or a Ferrari key ring, or a picture of Geraldine Ferraro. If they'd love to visit Paris, buy them a bag of French fries. You get the idea. At the time of the exchange, the giver should first read out what the recipient wished for, then say something like, "Well, I couldn't get you such and such, but will this do?" It's bound to be fun, since all the gifts are guaranteed to be gags! And maybe you still haven't found the world's greatest idea for a Christmas gift exchange…but will this do?

THE "TIME ZONE" PARTY

New Year's Eve is probably the biggest party night of the entire year, yet things don't usually get crazy until the clock strikes midnight and we usher in the new year with a wild burst of celebrating. With a "Time Zone" party, however, you'll be able to capture that "midnight madness" seven, eight, nine, or more times in the course of the same party! And it's all because, quite simply, every hour the clock strikes midnight *somewhere!* If you start your New Year's Eve party at 6 p.m. Eastern Standard Time, you'll be just in time for midnight in Paris. Your guests can have a wild moment of celebration while shouting "A votre santé! Bonne Année!" (That's "Cheers! Happy New Year!" in French). At 7 p.m. EST it's time to help the English ring in the new year, so drink another toast and kiss anyone you fancy! By 8 p.m. EST, the new year has reached Greenland, so all the guests should rub noses. If your clock says 9, it says midnight in Rio de Janeiro, so form a conga line and shout, "Feliz Ano Novo!" ("Happy New Year!" in Portuguese.) So on and on, through all the time zones you'll party, celebrating each time the clock strikes midnight anywhere! Hard-core partyers will want to begin around 3 p.m. EST, when it's midnight in Dubai, and continue until the new year rolls into Honolulu at 5 a.m. EST!

Here are a couple of things you can do for fun while you wait for another midnight:

CRACK ME UP: This is a funny game where the whole idea is not to laugh. Each contestant must try to keep a straight face while all the other guests try (without touching him) to make him laugh. Set a time limit of five minutes and see if any contestant can hold out that long. If several manage to stifle themselves for five minutes, have a "sudden laugh" playoff.

BLACK BART: This another type of "crack-up" game. In this one, two players sit opposite each other with a bowl of chips or other munchies set between them. Each player must stare directly into his opponent's eyes and keep his gaze there at all times. Player #1 then says, "Black Bart, this town ain't big enough for the both of us." Player #2 replies, "Tex, this town *ain't* big enough for the both of us." Still looking each other in the eye, both players eat a potato chip. First player to laugh has to get out of town!

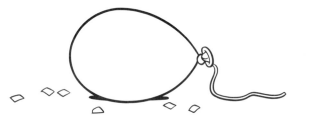

52

REASONS TO PARTY

Are you one of those people who actually needs a reason to party? Do you think lamp shades should only be worn on birthdays, anniversaries, and holidays? Do you sometimes go an entire week without doing something you should be ashamed of? If so, you *could* spend thousands of hours in costly "party therapy"; *or,* you could consult this list, guaranteed to provide you with a compelling reason to party every week of the year!

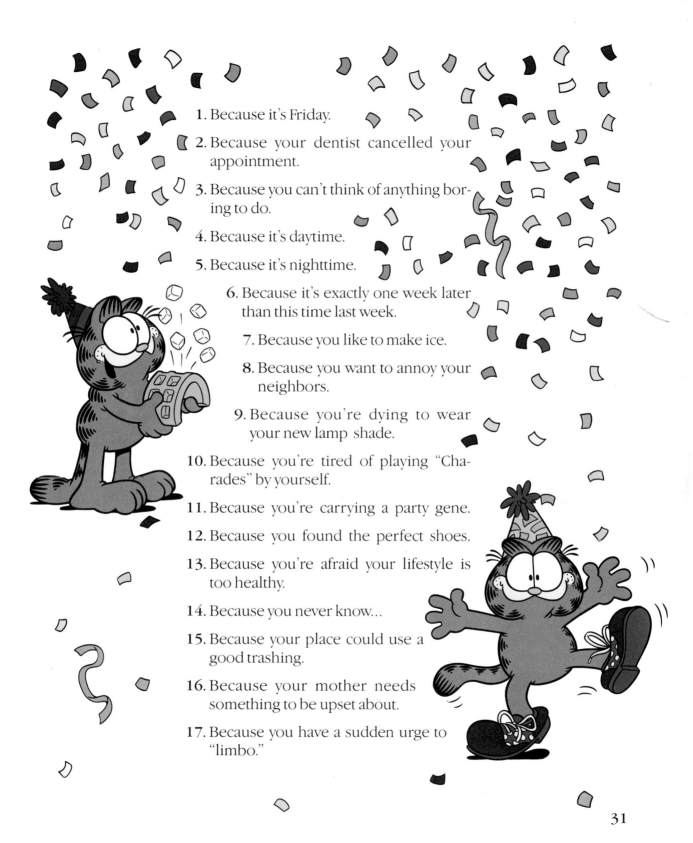

1. Because it's Friday.

2. Because your dentist cancelled your appointment.

3. Because you can't think of anything boring to do.

4. Because it's daytime.

5. Because it's nighttime.

6. Because it's exactly one week later than this time last week.

7. Because you like to make ice.

8. Because you want to annoy your neighbors.

9. Because you're dying to wear your new lamp shade.

10. Because you're tired of playing "Charades" by yourself.

11. Because you're carrying a party gene.

12. Because you found the perfect shoes.

13. Because you're afraid your lifestyle is too healthy.

14. Because you never know...

15. Because your place could use a good trashing.

16. Because your mother needs something to be upset about.

17. Because you have a sudden urge to "limbo."

18. Because your inhibitions are out of town.

19. Because the bank made an error in your favor.

20. Because it's there.

21. Because you need more bean dip in your diet.

22. Because the fun content of your blood is too low.

23. Because you look good doing it.

24. Because you're considering it as a career.

25. Because your yo-yo stock went up a point.

26. Because someone's got to do it.

27. Because you have a bad reputation to uphold.

28. Because your plants want to meet new people.

29. Because fun is a terrible thing to waste.

30. Because you want to try out your new coasters.

31. Because it's your patriotic duty.

32. Because you're going for the party record.

33. Because your roommate got rid of his scorpion farm.

34. Because you need the practice.

32

35. Because you're not getting any younger.

36. Because the vet says your hamster will pull through.

37. Because you've got it coming.

38. Because your life is starting to grow moss.

39. Because your brain needs a night off.

40. Because you never met a party you didn't like.

41. Because the fate of the free world depends on it.

42. Because the universe is expanding.

43. Because your dog is finally house-broken.

44. Because it's the only exercise you get.

45. Because maturity is overrated.

46. Because a party demon has possessed your body.

47. Because it hurts too much when you stop.

48. Because these are your "party years."

49. Because you're too polite to turn down an invitation.

50. Because you can't boogie to a book.

51. Because you have an over-active party gland.

52. Because the moon is in a party phase.

SPECIAL OCCASION PARTIES

or put the "stupid" back in birthday

Birthdays, anniversaries, graduations, retirement—these are milestones in our lives, when we gather with family and friends to mark the special significance of the moment by partying our brains out. In this chapter you'll find special parties for those special days, parties that add luster to the occasion, while they create memories that will last a lunchtime.

THE "GIFT THAT COUNTS" BIRTHDAY PARTY

It's a birthday tradition that the number of candles on the birthday cake should be equal to the age of the birthday person, which is why some people need a bonfire permit before they're allowed to celebrate their birthday. The "Gift That Counts" birthday party takes that tradition one step further by applying it, not only to the cake, but also to the gifts. Each guest must bring a gift that somehow represents the age of the birthday person. As an example, let's assume the birthday person has turned 24. Then your gift could be 24 dollars or 24 ping pong balls, or 24 of anything. It could be an athletic jersey bearing the number 24. Or it could be a 24 oz. jar of pickles, or two 12 oz. jars of pickles. Get the idea? Be creative. If a person was 16, you could get them a pool table (containing 15 numbered balls, plus a cue ball). Or look at the numbers in a different way. Think of 24 as "2" and "4," or a total of 6, and your 24th birthday gift could be a half-dozen doughnuts! The less obvious the connection, the more fun everyone will have trying to solve the puzzle!

35

THE "BARE MINIMUM" BIRTHDAY PARTY

There are all sorts of reasons for having a "Bare Minimum" birthday party. Maybe you haven't had time to organize a party, or you need a party that can be squeezed into a coffee break. Maybe you know that the birthday person really hates a lot of birthday fuss, or maybe the birthday person loves birthday fuss, and this is your way of zinging them. In any case, the "Bare Minimum" party is just that. Stick a match into a candy bar; there's your cake! Have everyone sign a single card; make it a used one, with the original signature scratched out. Give gifts like a roll of toilet paper (from the office bathroom, of course), a box of paper clips, or those little packets of sugar or catsup. (You can draw a bow on them, if you really feel like going to the trouble.) Sing "Happy Birthday," but only through the end of the first line. Go on about your business. It's a good way to show the birthday person that you cared enough to do the very least.

THE PHANTOM
BIRTHDAY PARTY

The essential requirement of this party is that you be able to enter the birthday person's home, office, or even car (in their absence, of course) without doing any damage or getting yourself arrested. Assuming that you have access, your task is to make it look like a party was held in the birthday person's place while they were away. So hang crepe paper streamers, then pull a few of them down, along with some partially-deflated balloons. Scatter confetti around the room. Place half-filled glasses and used plates and napkins on the tables, plus a cake plate containing the last few crumbs of cake and some burnt candles. A few pieces of clothing strewn here and there would make a nice additional touch. Then, once the room looks properly "partied," you leave a note for the birthday person that explains how you planned this great surprise party for them, and how everyone had a wild time, and how it's really too bad that the guest of honor had to miss the party. (Maybe you can even include a staged Polaroid of this "party" in progress.) Whether you then want to give this person a *real* party is entirely up to you. In any case, they might appreciate a little help cleaning up.

THE BIRTHDAY BUS BASH

This is what you might call a combination party/pilgrimage. You start off by noting all the places in or around town that mean something in the life of the birthday person. Likely spots would be the place the birthday person was born, schools they attended, places they have worked, where they picked up that rash, etc. Then you pile the guest of honor and everyone else into a rented bus and take the tour. Get off the bus at each location, explain its importance, wax nostalgic, boogie a little, and take off for the next party stop. Not only will this be a special treat for the birthday person (a sort of "This Is Your Life" on wheels), it also gives you the chance to move on before the neighbors get through to the police. If renting a bus proves too expensive, try a mini-van, or consider a caravan of cars. Bear in mind, though, that dancing will sometimes damage car upholstery.

THE "ONE FOOT IN THE GRAVE" PARTY

If someone you know has reached an age (such as 30) where they realize they're not going to live forever, then it's your responsibility as a friend or relative to add to their anxiety by driving this point home with a vengeance. With that in mind, decorate your place with plenty of black crepe. Have a sheet cake featuring black icing, cut in the shape of a tombstone. (And make it a bran cake; "old" people need that fiber!) Instead of the usual birthday greetings, ask the guests to bring sympathy cards, along with gifts like orthopedic stockings and denture cream. When you sing "Happy Birthday," make it sound slightly less cheery than a funeral dirge.

Of course, if you *really* want to drive home your point, you could hold this party in a funeral home. (They *can* be rented, you know, although funerals get priority.) Have a hearse pick up the birthday person, but keep the destination a secret. When the birthday person arrives at the funeral home, have the guests file in solemnly, wearing black armbands and carrying candles. Then conduct a mock service as if the birthday person had already "passed over." Have someone deliver a mock eulogy (with emphasis on the mock). Ask some of the "mourners" to say a few words. Then strike up the organ music, and party like there's no tomorrow!

THE "KIDDY" BIRTHDAY PARTY

This is one birthday party that actually encourages childish behavior. The idea is to re-create one of those kiddy birthday parties you went to when you were, well, a kid. (If you never went to one, here's your big chance.) All the guests should wear party hats and be given party favors like horns and blow-outs (you know, those things that uncurl like a lizard's tongue when you blow into them). Play kids' games like "Pin the Tail on the Donkey." and the "Clothespin Drop" (into a glass juice bottle, as hardly anyone puts milk in bottles these days). And don't forget those classic relay race games, such as sticking an orange under your chin and attempting to pass it to a teammate without using your hands; racing across a room with a raw egg balanced on a teaspoon; or the "Balloon Bust" game, where you take a balloon, race to a chair, pop the balloon by sitting on it, then race back to tag your teammate. For presents and prizes, give those cheap little trinkets (jacks, yo-yos, paddleballs, kaleidoscopes, etc.) that you loved as a kid. Everyone should be allowed to yell, giggle, whine, and generally act like a six-year-old, provided they also play nice, drink their milk with both hands, and don't stick things up their noses.

THE "WHAT A COINCIDENCE!" BIRTHDAY SURPRISE

Here's a birthday surprise party that develops gradually and relies a lot on the ability of the *guests* to feign surprise. It works like this: You take the birthday person out for dinner, or an ice cream, or an oil change, or something. When you reach your destination, who should you run into, but a couple of mutual friends! They join you. After a while, someone suggests that you all go to another place (roller rink, bowling alley, whatever). While you're there—what a coincidence!—you run into *more* friends! After a short while, it's decided that you should all adjourn to yet another location, where you are "surprised" to meet the last of your fellow conspirators. At this point the surprise is announced to the (hopefully) still-in-the-dark guest of honor. (Three or four "coincidental" meetings is probably the most you can get away with, unless the birthday person has the perspicuity of a doorknob.) Then it's time to start the party!

Another way to arrange this sort of "snowballing" party would be to take the birthday person to dinner at a restaurant atop a high-rise building (a hotel is ideal). Then have your fellow conspirators board your elevator at different floors, until you have a surprise party of ten to twelve people by the time you reach the top!

41

THE BIRTHDAY
"WEEK OF PARTIES"

As Garfield always says, "Anything worth doing is worth overdoing!" Instead of the usual one-day birthday celebration, plan an entire week of fun, with a different type of party each night! You could start with a formal dinner party, followed by a pool party, followed the next night by a tailgate party, and so on, all leading up to a big birthday party. Or lead off with the birthday party, and follow it with six different and interesting alternatives. (You shouldn't have any trouble coming up with alternative party ideas, now that you've so wisely invested in this book.) Consider giving the birthday person a present each day. It could be something appropriate for that night's celebration, e.g., a spinning bow tie for the formal dinner party, or a fake shark fin for the pool party. Or perhaps you could give a gift that comes in seven different parts. Like dwarfs, for instance. Or a golf ball per day for six days, topped off by a new set of clubs on the seventh. If you do give some gifts which are the same (like golf balls) wrap them in different size boxes, so each one will appear to be something different.

Bear in mind that after seven consecutive nights of partying, you will need to "party down" with a few more sedate social functions before you resume your regular routine. Cutting off the parties too abruptly could trigger a severe bout of post-party depression.

42

THE "BLAST FROM THE PAST" BIRTHDAY PARTY

All of us could name certain people from our past whom we would love to see again. People who still owe us money, for instance. But we'd also like to be reunited with a favorite teacher, a childhood friend who moved away, or a college roommate we somehow lost track of.

The "Blast From the Past" party challenges you to identify these people from the past whom the birthday person would be pleasantly surprised to see again. Once you've identified these people, then you'll need to locate them (through the phone book, mutual acquaintances, college alumni offices, etc.). If you can manage to contact them, and they're willing and able to attend the party, then your next challenge is deciding how to spring them on the birthday person.

One simple way would be for each "blast" to come to the door at a specified time. Have the birthday person answer the door on each occasion, while everyone else stand back to watch the surprise! Wondering who's coming next, and when they'll arrive, will keep the birthday person in suspense all evening! (When the last "blast" has arrived, be kind enough to tell the birthday person not to expect any more.)

Another approach would be to blindfold the birthday person and bring in the "blasts" one at a time. Have each surprise guest relate an anecdote about the birthday person and see if the birthday person can recognize them from the story and voice. This will be even more fun if some of the other guests (or better yet, people unknown to the birthday person) take the parts of fictitious characters from the birthday person's past. Have someone pose as the birthday person's former prison cellmate. Introduce an abandoned former spouse. The birthday person will go crazy trying to identify these people!

If the "blast" is fairly limber and not a whole lot bigger than a breadbox, it's also possible to wrap them up as a surprise package. To do this, wrap a large box which has had the bottom cut off. Then have the "blast" curl up on a counter or table, and slip the box over them. (This won't be extremely comfortable, so make sure the package is opened quickly. You might even want to add a few airholes.) The birthday person will wonder what can be in this large package, and probably the last thing they'd expect to find is the kid who sat behind them in health class!

THE "COME AS YOU WERE" ANNIVERSARY PARTY

Couples celebrating a wedding anniversary are bound to be thinking about the past, so here's an anniversary party idea that positively reeks of nostalgia.

Inform the happy couple and all the guests that you intend to re-create, as much as possible, the year in which the couple married. Everyone, including the anniversary couple, should wear the clothes and hairstyles of that era. (If the anniversary couple still have, and can still wear, their original wedding clothes, that would be ideal!) Make a special effort to invite members of the original wedding party and guests from the wedding. Set the mood by playing music of that era throughout the party. Chauffeuring the wedding couple in a car of that era would be a nice touch. Decorate with copies of front pages, sports pages, and comics pages from newspapers of the day. (These can usually be obtained from the library or from the newspaper itself.) And don't forget to set out old wedding (and other) pictures of the anniversary couple, their relatives, and friends.

If the anniversary couple would really love to "do it all over again," they could actually get married again, perhaps in the same church, synagogue, judge's chambers, etc., where they were originally married. If the original wedding reception was held in a place large enough to accommodate the current guests, you might want to see if it is available for a wedding reception sequel!

THE ANNIVERSARY DOCUMENTARY PARTY

What is an anniversary? A time for memories...a time for renewal...a time for love...but most of all, a time to make fun of the happy couple.

This idea requires a bit of effort and planning on your part, but the results are practically guaranteed to be a hit. Start by locating a book filled with pictures from old movies. Make slides (or a videotape) of pictures which suggest imaginary scenes from the life of the anniversary couple. (Movie stills from silent movies are often very campy and will suggest funny captions.) Then add a humorous narration to go with the slides or tape. For instance, if you have an old picture of a surprised woman being grabbed by a gorilla, your narration might be something like, "From the very beginning of their courtship, Bob was always the complete gentleman." Or, "Mary was impressed with Bob's physique, but she did wish he would shave a little closer." When you're finished, you have a pseudo-documentary of the happy couple's marriage. You can even include actual photos of the couple in your documentary, as the real thing is often just as funny as the fake. The screening of your masterpiece will be the highlight of the anniversary party.

If you can't manage the slides or videotape, you can easily create a funny anniversary photo album to present to the happy couple. This can involve real pictures of the couple, their friends and their relatives, with each picture featuring a funny caption; or you can take pictures from magazines and have them serve as "family photos." Thus, a photo of a group of chimps could be "Bob, Mary, and the kids enjoy an outing in the jungles of Indiana."

THE
"BABY'S 21st BIRTHDAY"
SHOWER

First of all, if you'd like your baby shower to be something *really* different, all you need to do is invite men. More men than ever before are taking more interest in babies, besides which they are useful for carrying heavy things like playpens.

For the "Baby's 21st Birthday" shower, you'll need a video camera. If you don't have one, surely you know someone who does. Then, at the party, you tape each guest speaking to the camera as if he or she were addressing the baby. The guest should predict what this baby will be like 21 years in the future. For instance, "Hello, Jeff. Yes, I think you're going to be a boy. I bet you'll have your mother's nose and brains, and your father's hair and sense of humor. I think you like basketball and baseball, and just graduated summa cum laude from Harvard with a degree in history, and you're going on to grad school." You can also include predictions about life in general, such as, "I think you'll be driving electric cars, postage will be two dollars per letter, and Sylvester Stallone will be president of the United States." When all the predictions have been given, the tape should be securely stored, to be given to the baby on his or her 21st birthday, when you should collect as many of the original guests as possible, and see how accurate they were!

If you'd like to do something a little less high-tech, why not make a time capsule for the baby? Ask each guest to bring (along with a normal present) something of personal or general interest. It could be a note for the baby, or a newspaper clipping, or a photograph of the baby's parents. These items should then be carefully sealed in a container, and presented to the baby at some future date, like a 21st birthday, graduation day, etc.

THE "KEEP 'EM BUSY" RETIREMENT BASH

People who retire are suddenly faced with an abundance of free time. To fill up this time, some retirees start collecting things like coins or driftwood. Too many, however, simply start collecting dust. It is vitally important for our society that these retirees remain occupied, otherwise they will hang out on street corners, join gangs, and be drawn into a life of crime.

The purpose of this party, then, is for the guests to provide the retirees with things that will help fill up the retiree's free time. The possibilities here are practically endless. You could give something simple, like a book or a model ship kit. But you might want to strike a more active, upbeat note by giving jogging shoes or dancing lessons. What about an entertainment book filled with coupons for restaurants, movies, museums, the zoo, etc? Consider fishing, golfing and gardening equipment. Groups of people could chip in on an exercise bike, health club membership, or luggage (complete with travel brochures). Give them a calendar that includes an activity for each day, even if it's only something like "Check underwear for boll weevils." Remember, if you don't provide ways to keep these people busy, they may come back to the office and start bothering *you!*

THE GRADUATION "BIG DEAL"

Graduating from high school, college, or professional school is a very important event in the life of any young person, so give them a graduation party that they'll never forget, no matter how hard they try!

Start by having all the guests line up to shower the graduate with confetti as he or she walks down a path to a special "throne of honor" (which can be something as simple as a lawn chair decorated with ribbons). This is followed by a short ceremony. Read out fake telegrams of congratulations from important people, e.g., "I lost my shirt on this one, but congrats anyway. Jimmy the Greek." If the graduate does not have a job lined up, the telegrams can also include phony job offers, e.g., "We believe that your years in college have made you exceptionally well-qualified for a position with our firm. Come see us. The Acme Party Supply Company." If the graduate's future plans are already known, you could present him with gag gifts that will assist him in his career. Someone going into dentistry could receive a pair of pliers, or a hammer and chisel "for those really tough patches of plaque," while someone going on for more schooling could receive clean underwear and pizza coupons. When all the gags have been read, the guests should file past the graduate and offer their congratulations. If you have any influence with local TV stations, see if you can get a camera crew out to film the event and interview the graduate. (They don't necessarily have to air it, just film it for your amusement.) Top things off with a fireworks display, or a plane bearing a message of congratulations for the graduate.

are you a party animal?

What is a party animal?

A party animal is just your average party-goer who likes to swing from chandeliers and spit olives at the other guests. It's some-one who knows the meaning of the word "booga," but not the word "decorum." A party animal looks at life through Groucho glasses, and knows that any time is the right time to party!

Who knows? A party animal could be someone just like you! To find out, take this quick quiz specifically designed to measure your P.A.P. (Party Animal Potential)!

1. Your idea of a party is...

    A. a tax seminar
    B. showing home movies to friends
    C. Carnival time in Rio...only wilder

2. When you go to a party, you usually bring...

    A. a good book
    B. a bag of pretzels
    C. bail money

3. The first thing you do at a party is...

    A. check what's on TV
    B. mingle with the other guests
    C. smash something against your forehead and belch

4. Your favorite party game is...

    A. "Name That Molecular Structure"
    B. "Twenty Questions"
    C. "Let's Smash Something Against Our Foreheads and Belch"

5. Your idea of proper party attire is...

    A. a pocket protector filled with your best pencils
    B. a nice sweater and slacks
    C. a lamp shade, fake nose, and edible underwear

6. You think the perfect party menu should include...

    A. milk and cookies
    B. cheese and crackers
    C. foods that explode when you throw them against the wall

7. You think people should party...

    A. once a year

    B. once a month

    C. once they wake up

8. If you break something at a party, you usually...

    A. lock yourself in the bathroom

    B. offer to pay for it

    C. scrape it off your forehead and belch

9. Your favorite type of party music is...

    A. Gregorian chant

    B. Broadway show tunes

    C. loud

10. You usually leave a party...

    A. about 9 p.m.

    B. about 1 a.m.

    C. face down

HOW TO SCORE

Give yourself 1 point for each A answer; 2 points for each B answer; and 3 points for each C answer.

10–15 points: When it comes to partying, you obviously don't get the concept. Get rich, and hire others to party for you.

15–20 points: You have only marginal P.A.P., but may find your niche in square dancing.

20–25 points: Very promising. With a little extra effort you could soon be behaving disgracefully.

25–30 points: Why are you wasting valuable party time on this quiz, you party animal?!

Everyday Parties

-or-

It's Tuesday, let's boogie!

Now that you've learned all about holiday and special-occasion parties, it's time you were introduced to a higher level of celebrating, i.e. partying for the sake of partying! After all, no true party animal is going to confine his activities to those all-too-few official party days. So here are suggestions for parties you can have whenever you're in a party mood. And if you're not sure when that is, just remember this: When in doubt, party!

THE BALLOON BLOWOUT

WHAT YOU'LL NEED:

Balloons, lots of them

Air, lots of it, for inflating the balloons

One or more rooms devoid of sharp objects

*Steady nerves, for withstanding sudden,
loud bangs without dropping plates of food*

Remove all the sharp and hot objects from a room. Inflate the balloons (a tank of air might be a good investment here) and fill the room with balloons. And we do mean *fill!* The balloons should reach at least to the chin of the shortest guest you're expecting, and high enough so that walking is like fording a river of balloons! Add the guests, warning the smokers and those with spiked hair to be especially cautious. Mix well. At midnight, encourage everyone to start popping balloons, preferably by smashing them between bodies!

55

THE SLUMBER PARTY

WHAT YOU'LL NEED:

Pillows, blankets, sleeping bags, air mattresses, water beds, etc.

Several gallons of warm milk

Bedtime reading material, such as Paradise Lost, *or other writings likely to induce drowsiness*

Space for all your guests to lie down

Pajamas (optional)

As Garfield might say, "Too much sleep is not enough," and in these hectic times too many of us are sleeping too little. So why not combine a little entertainment with a little rest by throwing a slumber party? It's a slumber party, however, with this crucial difference: instead of staying up all night giggling, talking, and eating fudge, at this party you actually sleep! If your guests can't doze off without a favorite pillow or blanket, tell them to bring it along. You might even want to make the party BYOTB (Bring Your Own Teddy Bear). Set the mood by dimming the lights and playing a relaxation tape as your guests sip warm milk. When you hear the snores, you'll know your party is a success! This is the one party where you'll probably be in better shape when you leave than when you arrived!

MUDSLIDE MANIA
WHAT YOU'LL NEED:

A long, muddy, rock-free slope, preferably one declining to a large, muddy, rock-free puddle of water

Old clothes, plus a change of clothing

A willingness to throw cleanliness to the winds

If you like to get down and roll around in your fun, the "Mudslide Mania" party is for you! All you need is a hill, a hole, and enough water to make a mess of it! (If you happen to be putting in a pool or a new basement, you probably have all the ingredients.) Once the "slide" has been properly slicked, you need to get a running start, then launch yourself on your back, bottom, belly, knees, or whatever, down the "slide" and into the waller at the bottom! You can also make the trip on an inner tube, although body slides seem to work best. Vote on best individual slides, giving extra style points to those who go face first. Try gang sliding. You'll want to keep a garden hose handy for "slide-slopping" and guest cleanup. And it really doesn't matter what foods you serve, as most of the guests won't be able to taste anything except mud.

NERD NIGHT
WHAT YOU'LL NEED:

Nerdwear (white shirt, pants several inches too short, white socks, black shoes)

Thick, horn-rimmed glasses

Pocket calculator, preferably programmable

Nerdfood (bologna and catsup sandwiches, vanilla wafers, broccoli, fruit pies)

Button your white shirt tight against your Adam's apple, hike up your pants, and get ready to let your cowlick down with a "Nerd Night"! This is one party where you'll actually be applauded for acting like a geek! Divide your guests into teams and see who can find the most prime numbers! Tell jokes in Latin! Show a Jerry Lewis film! No one admitted without a pocket protector and tape on their glasses!

THE FILM FESTIVAL

WHAT YOU'LL NEED:

*Several TVs and VCRs (these can be
your own, borrowed, brought by the guests,
or even rented)*

Movies on videocassette

Tons of popcorn

Each year the city of Cannes on the French Riviera hosts a film festival which features movie stars, movie moguls, the world press, thousands of autograph seekers, multi-million-dollar deals, and wild parties filled with beautiful people. It's a glittering, glamorous, decadent, and incredibly exciting romp in the Mediterranean sun.

Unfortunately, *your* film festival won't be anything like that. But that doesn't mean you can't have fun! Start by picking a theme. Your film festival could focus on a specific genre (westerns, horror films, musicals, etc.), or on the works of a specific actor or director. Once you've chosen a theme, tell your guests that they must each bring a favorite film that fits the theme. (Have them communicate their choices to you, so there's less chance of duplication.) On festival night, set up all the VCRs and TVs in the same room. That way everyone can view all the films at once, and you won't miss the "good parts" from any movie. Just imagine a martial arts film festival where you can watch "Fists of Fury," "Feet of Fury," "Face of Fury," "Femurs of Fury," and "Follicles of Fury" all at the same time! That's something you'll certainly never see at Cannes!

THE WADING POOL PARTY

WHAT YOU'LL NEED:

Kids' wading pools

Water

Suntan lotion

Just because you don't have a built-in, kidney-shaped pool on your heavily mortgaged estate, that doesn't mean you can't invite the gang over for a pool party...provided they bring their own pools. Tell each guest to bring a child's wading pool. Then push all of them together in your yard, fill with water, and yell, "Everyone into the pools!" Play a game of volleyball with a rule that each player must stay in his own little pool. Try paddling from pool to pool on an air mattress. See how many people you can get in a single pool. All it takes is a little sun, a little water, and a little imagination, and you'll soon be up to your ankles in fun!

THE FRIDAY THE 13TH FÊTE

WHAT YOU'LL NEED:

One Friday the 13th

Unlucky stuff

Guests (13 would be an appropriately inauspicious number)

Celebrate ignorant superstitions by daring to throw a party on the unluckiest day of all! Place a ladder inside your front door and force your guests to walk under it as they enter. Sprinkle your place with black cats. Open umbrellas inside the house. Play games like "Mirror Toss," or "Don't Cry Over Spilled Salt," where you have to walk across the room with a salt shaker balanced on your head. Or stage a scene from Shakespeare's *Macbeth*, long considered by actors to be an unlucky play. Maybe you'll get lucky and have fun, but if the party's a bomb, you can always say it was doomed from the start!

THE TOURIST WINGDING

WHAT YOU'LL NEED:

*Touristwear (loud shirts,
Bermuda shorts, stretch pants, straw hats,
sunglasses, camera bags)*

Luggage

Passports

Frozen dinners

The proper shots

This is the perfect party for people who always travel worst-class. Guests should dress like the typical tourist and be as loud and obnoxious as possible. Have everyone bring a piece of luggage, and see who can carry the most pieces at one time. Decorate your place with travel posters and any souvenirs you've acquired along the way, even if it's only your dysentery medicine. For refreshments, serve partially thawed TV dinners. (These will simulate airline food, which is meant to simulate real food.) Don't admit anyone without a camera, and make certain the guests take plenty of pictures of each other. And whatever you do, don't drink the water!

If you like, you can choose to focus your "Tourist Wingding" on a specific location, e.g., Italy. Then the entire party would have an Italian flair. Your guests would dine on pasta, Italian opera music would pour from the stereo, posters of Rome and Florence would festoon the walls, and everyone would ask directions to the bathroom in bad Italian.

63

THE BARBARIAN BASH

WHAT YOU'LL NEED:

Long wooden table (picnic tables or even a door on sawhorses will do)

Maces, shields, helmets, animal skins, or any other barbarian accoutrements

Large drinking cups (drinking horns would be even better; check your local barbarian supplies outlet)

Wenches

Here's a throwback to the good old days when no one cared if you cut your meat with a battleax. Tell your friends to dig up some barbarian wear and join you for an evening of lusty dining! Set the table in the mead hall. (If your mead hall is already booked, try your garage, or the backyard.) Serve foods which can be torn apart with the hands and have plenty of bones you can throw, such as roast chicken or pig. You can serve the food on plates, especially if you don't mind people breaking them, but don't bother with napkins. Make elaborate toasts, boast about your exploits, gulp your drinks, and talk with your mouth full. Always slap your thighs as you roar with laughter. For after-dinner entertainment, you might throw an ax at a target. Or better yet, pillage a small town!

THE UGLY TIE PARTY

WHAT YOU'LL NEED:

Ugly ties

Extra batteries (for those ties that require them)

Guests who know bad taste when they're wearing it

Let's break out the nauseating neckwear and tie one on! Here's a chance to use that purple and orange polka dot monstrosity that's been moldering in the back of your tie drawer since Christmas, 1972. No guest (male or female) will be admitted to the party unless they are sporting a tie that looks like a hamster got sick on it. Guests who have an ugly suit to go with their ugly tie will be especially welcome. Have an "Ugliest Tie" contest, giving special consideration to those ties which are hand-painted, illuminated, or wide enough to make into a hang glider.

Of course, once you've gone to all the trouble of being so poorly dressed, it seems a shame not to share your fashion statement with the public. If you get the opportunity, stick your neck out at a mall or supermarket. When you're certain that people are staring, pretend to blow your nose in the tie.

65

THE "BASH" BASH
WHAT YOU'LL NEED:

Bashers
Something to bash with
Something to bash

One of the necessary elements of any great party is the destruction of property. It's a tradition that goes back at least as far as the Huns, who trashed the Roman Empire (and consequently were never invited back). But the idea behind the "Bash" Bash is that you have something you want to destroy, either for practical reasons or simply for the fun of it. For instance, maybe you have an old piano you wouldn't mind pulverizing. Better still, buy an old junker car and have it towed to your place. Then get your friends together, break out the sledgehammers, and start bashing away! You'll find that some people who can barely work a zipper have a real flair for destruction. Just be certain that everyone has plenty of room to swing, and that you take precautions against flying splinters. When the bashing's done, you can have the debris hauled away. Or simply leave it in your yard and tell visitors that it's the latest in modern birdbaths.

THE PROM PARTY

WHAT YOU'LL NEED:

Promwear (tuxedos for men, formal gowns for women)

Flowers (corsages for the women, boutonnieres for the men)

Prom decorations

Music

Room to dance

Bathroom large enough for all the women to fix their makeup at the same time

Here it is! Your chance to recapture all the thrills, romance, awkwardness, sweaty palms, embarrassment, sore toes, and acne of those wonderful high school days! The fun starts when your "Prom Decoration Committee" arrives early in the day to bedeck your place with crepe paper and cute little table decorations. (At this time all the women on the decorating committee should be wearing hair curlers the size of fifty-gallon drums.) Be sure to hang a silver reflecting ball over the dance floor.

The happy couples should arrive around eightish. If you've chosen a particular year for your prom—say, "Prom Night, 1963"—then everyone should dress for that year, and the music should be the music of that time. If you can arrive in cars of that era, so much the better. The high point of the festivities, of course, will be the selection of the prom king and queen, who should shuffle around the floor to the strains of your "prom theme."

Tell all the guests to bring their high school yearbooks, so that when you get tired of dancing (after all, you're not kids anymore), you can amuse and humiliate each other with the photographic evidence of your "geek years." Just be certain not to stay out too late, or you might be forced to ground yourself.

THE NOVELTY PARTY
WHAT YOU'LL NEED:

Dribble glasses, whoopee cushions, onion gum, chattering teeth, joy buzzers, phony dog doo, snakes in a can, Groucho glasses, phony arrows through the head, squirting carnations, and any other novelty item you think is good for a laugh

If it's sophisticated, adult entertainment you're looking for, boy, have you come to the wrong party! The Novelty Party is a celebration of our eternal search for the cheap laugh. No home should be without at least one novelty item. Tell your guests to bring along their favorite, and let the laughs begin! See who'll be the first to fall victim to the dreaded dribble glass! Watch your guests swoon at the sight of the rubber snake! And everyone will get a charge out of the joy buzzers! Don't forget to serve phony, bug-filled ice cubes and rubber hot dogs. And a word of advice: Don't invite anyone who doesn't have the stomach for plastic barf.

Though this party has been included in the Everyday Parties section of this book, there *is* a specific day of the year for which it is perfectly suited: April Fool's Day!

THE "SOMETHING IN COMMON" SOIRÉE

WHAT YOU'LL NEED:

A group of people who share some common trait, interest, occupation, etc.

A good retirement plan (not for this party, but it never hurts to think about your future)

Invite a bunch of people to your party, tell them that they all have something in common, and let them try to discover what it is! The common trait can be anything, and the possibilities are endless. All it takes is a little research and/or careful observation on your part. For instance, all the guests could have brown eyes, or big noses, or both! Maybe they're all lefthanded. Maybe they all went to the same college, or they've all seen Rock City. Maybe all they have in common is that they never pass up a party! Let *them* figure it out!

THE PIE FIGHT PARTY
WHAT YOU'LL NEED:

Paper plates or foil pie plates

Numerous cans of whipped cream

*Enough plastic sheeting to cover your
entire home and all your possessions*

Partying took a giant step forward the first time someone took a pie in the face. Throughout history all of the world's most renowned partyers have been "pied." King Henry VIII, for example, was pasted with a large banana cream pie thrown by his second wife, Anne Boleyn. Henry found this so amusing that he had Anne beheaded.

If you would like to keep this great party tradition alive, all you need do is squirt a pile of whipped cream onto a paper plate, select your target, and fire away! Once the first missile has been launched, there's no turning back, and the air should soon be thick with megacalorie warheads. The fight could take the form of a mêlée, where it's every thrower for himself, or you could consider organizing the guests into two hostile camps, each with makeshift barricades. See if you can devise slings and catapults for long-range bombardment. And when peace reigns once more, bring out the ingredients for ice cream sundaes and banana splits so that you can eat up your arsenal. Or throw those, too, if you like! This is one party that's bound to be a direct hit!

THE MAKE-A-MOVIE PARTY

WHAT YOU'LL NEED:

Video camera

Background music

Actors, writers, directors, assistant directors, producers, associate producers, casting directors, set designers, costume designers, camerapersons, cinematographers, sound engineers, editors, lighting people, makeup artists, gaffers, grips, best boys, stunt people, wranglers, accountants, teamsters, and someone to make the popcorn, or maybe just a few friends

Most home videos look the same: people sitting, people standing, people waving, people smiling nervously at the camera, people eating, people eating nervously while sitting and waving at the camera. In other words, Snoozeville. So why not try something more ambitious, interesting, and fun, like your own mini-movie spectacular? First, you'll need to create a plot and write some dialogue. That shouldn't take more than an hour. Select a director, cast, and location, and you're all ready to roll the cameras! Don't forget to include appropriate background music, remind the actors not to say "Should I start? You mean now?" every time you say "Action!," and try not to go more than $10 million over budget.

When you've finished shooting, you *could* view the results right away; or, wait until you've edited the film, and added titles and credits, and then screen it at a special premiere party!

Another interesting variation on this idea would be to make your own music video version of one of your favorite songs.

THE ALTERNATIVE FASHIONS FÊTE

WHAT YOU'LL NEED:

Something—anything—to wear

The nerve to wear it

Just when you think you've worn it all, here's a party that shows you how to turn kitchenware into kitchenwear! The idea is for all the guests to come dressed in party outfits that they have created themselves. The catch is, these outfits must be created from something other than clothing. (For purposes of comfort and safety, shoes will be acceptable, particularly if they are worn someplace other than the feet.) Try to steer people away from obvious solutions like sheets and towels. What you're looking for is real ingenuity! How about a garbage bag and tin foil ensemble? Or what if you wrapped yourself in multiple layers of toilet paper? Could you make a pair of pants using magazine pages and a stapler? Even a small appliance could serve as proper attire, provided it was strategically placed. When all the guests have arrived, organize an alternative fashion show and vote on the most creative apparel. Some of the fashions will be so bizarre they could easily pass for Paris originals! One thing's for certain: Once you've been to this party, never again will you be able to say that you don't have anything to wear!

73

THE "ART CHALLENGE" PARTY

WHAT YOU'LL NEED:

Art (the kind you make yourself)
A place to display art
Space to perform art
Art appreciators

Many people have artistic skills which they love to show off. Many more have artistic potential which they have never had the opportunity, or the nerve, to develop. Here's a party that showcases everyone's peculiar (sometimes *very* peculiar) artistic ability. Each guest must bring a work of art that they have created to the party. Ideally, this should be something you've created in the recent past, although the ashtray you made at summer camp will do in a pinch. Your exhibit could be a painting, sculpture, or ceramic piece you made. It could be a story, poem, or song you wrote. You could play the piano, accordian, or spoons. Tap dance. Make shadow pictures on the wall. If you excel at the art of cooking or baking, bring in one of your culinary creations! The main idea is for you to express some side of yourself which many of your friends may not even be aware of! All creations should be prominently displayed or performed. This is bound to be entertaining, and it may even encourage some people to pursue their artistic interest. Besides which, you could wind up with a stunning, black velvet painting of an old sea dog to hang in your living room!

THE LAMP SHADE PARTY
WHAT YOU'LL NEED:

A lamp shade

A party

Gloves, purse, and shoes to match

Sure, we all have this mental image of a rowdy party animal boogieing across the coffee table with a lamp shade tilting crazily atop his head. But when was the last time you actually *saw* someone at a party wearing a lamp shade? Is this treasured piece of partyana going the way of other party fun, like bearbaiting? Let's try to breathe new life into this time-honored tradition! Throw a party where all the guests are expected to bring and wear their own lamp shade. (Shades from bedside lamps should work very well.) Want to show them that you're a *real* party animal? Wear the entire lamp!

THE SURPRISE PARTY

WHAT YOU'LL NEED:

*All the fixings for a party, since you can't
expect the "host" to have them*

People to join you in the surprise

Someone to surprise

When people hear the words "surprise party," they immediately think of a birthday or other special occasion. But why does it have to be a birthday party? Why not surprise someone by deciding to hold a party at their place, only they don't know it? The first thing you need to do, of course, is make sure that the "host" will be home on that particular evening. You might also want to make certain that this person has not already planned some important home activity that evening, such as a romantic dinner with a new love interest, or shellacking all the floors. Then, you and the other guest-conspirators should arrive at the same time, laden with all the goodies you'll need for a party. Ring the doorbell, and when the "host" answers say, "Somebody here order a party?" or "Partygram!" If the door is immediately slammed in your face or your "host" turns a firehose on you, then you've probably picked a bad night. But if you can just manage to get your cheeseball in the door, the party will be off and running!

THE PARLOR GAMES PENTATHLON

WHAT YOU'LL NEED:

Chess or checker set

Deck of cards

Trivia game

Dictionary

Board game

Tote board

An even number of players

Here's a party for fierce competitors that will force them to stretch their minds to the limit, while their bodies sit comfortably in chairs and scarf pretzel rods. This is a five-event competition (pentathlon) consisting of:

1) chess or checkers
2) a card game (make it one with a definite endpoint, such as "Hearts")
3) a trivia game
4) a word game (pick a seven-letter word and see who can form the most words of at least three letters from it within ten minutes)
5) any board game most of you enjoy playing that doesn't take more than thirty minutes to an hour.

Depending on the size of the party, more than one competition will probably be going on at the same time. Each person who wins a game, either as an individual or a member of a team, receives one point, with a half-point being awarded for a tie. As the events are completed, be sure to keep a running tally on a tote board so everyone can keep track of the leaders. The person with the most overall points at the end of the evening is the winner. In the event of a tie, there should be a mutually agreed upon "checker-off," "Hearts-off," or "whatever-off." The winner should graciously accept the congratulations of the losers, then leave before things get ugly.

77

THE GRAFFITI PARTY

WHAT YOU'LL NEED:

A large wall, sheet, piece of canvas, or anything else you won't mind defacing

Marking pens or spray paint

Guests who have something to say

Man's need to express himself with graffiti is as old as he is. The earliest extant examples have been found on bathroom stalls and public phone booths dating from the ninth millenium B.C. A "Graffiti Party" will allow you to unleash this primal urge. Simply decide what it is you want to deface, be it a wall or an old washing machine. (The larger the object, the better, of course.) Then provide your guests with marking pens or spray cans and encourage them to create a memorial for all time. It doesn't matter what they write or draw. Some of it will be profound. Some of it is likely to be profane. But, in the tradition of graffiti writing, it should all be anonymous (or at least pseudonymous). Your guests can have a lot of fun writing and reading, and when it's over, you'll have an unusual souvenir of the party!

THE BLACKOUT PARTY

WHAT YOU'LL NEED:

Total darkness

Flashlights

*A keen sense of hearing, smell,
taste and touch*

We've all had some great times in the dark, but for this one you'll want to stay awake. This is a party that doesn't want to be seen, so tell all your guests to arrive after sunset. Then pull the shades, kill the lights, and let the fun begin! Hardcore "blackout" partyers will want to grope along in the dark, but you can also achieve some interesting effects with black lights or strobe lights. Or consider providing each guest with a phosphorescent patch or button. (In any case, it's probably wise to keep a few flashlights handy, and make sure any hazardous areas, like stairs, are clearly marked.) Threads hanging in a doorway will give people a creepy cobweb sensation as they walk through. And this is an excellent time to coat those doorknobs with shaving cream. While you're at it, booby-trap the buffet with a few fake food items! If you really want great results, hold this party on a moonless night in your basement. Or rent a cave.

how to KILL a PARTY

t's a tough business, hosting a party. One minute your bash is a million laughs, a carnival, a prison riot . . . you get the picture. And the next minute, Morgue City. When a party dies, it's not a pretty sight. And it can happen faster than you can say, "More cheese puffs?". If you want to kiss off the fun at your next party, just be stupid enough to try any of the following:

- Show slides of your dog
- Describe, in graphic detail, how you had your polyps removed
- Force people to guess the scientific names of your plants
- Ration the refreshments

  - Impose a curfew
  - Have your children perform, especially if they don't want to
    - Organize a sensitivity session
    - Hold your party next door to a slaughterhouse
    - Invite a group of Hari Krishnas
- Serve nothing but wheat germ and carrot juice
- Instead of playing party games, ask your guests to refinish your dinette set
- Read from your unpublished book of accounting anecdotes
- Use food coloring to turn all the food blue

  - Ask everyone to join you in a moment of silence for all those less fortunate than yourselves
  - Announce that your plumbing is out of order
- Do finger shadows on the wall
- Explain the fine points of your scissors collection
- Ask if anyone knows the symptoms of food poisoning
- Weep uncontrollably

mini-
parties

or
It's not the size of the party, but the fun, that counts.

You are about to enter a new realm of partying, a place where you don't need a crowd of people and bags of ice and a buffet to have a good time. You are about to enter the "Mini-Party Zone". A mini-party is something you do when the day is dull and you crave amusement. It's something you can do for yourself or with a few others. It can be as simple as placing a mirror on your living room floor and getting a new perspective on your apartment. Or maybe you put on an animal costume, stand in your front yard, and wave at the passing cars. It doesn't really matter what you do, as long as you do it for fun!

This chapter contains suggestions for ways to put a little "party" in your day. Once you get the concept, you're bound to come up with plenty of your own!

PARTIES AROUND THE HOUSE

If you're on your own, it's fun to go around the house and do things your parents never let you do, e.g., jump on your bed, walk on the furniture, eat with your mouth open, scrape your fingernails on the screen door, and run down the hallway screaming like a banshee.

The phone directory is a great source of entertainment. Find funny names (Rosco Moose, Matilda Trout, C. Sharp, etc.). Find famous names (Pearl Bailey, Clark Gable, George Washington, etc.). As an interesting variation, find names in the obituary section of the newspaper, then go to the phone book and cross them off.

Discover a new smell, taste, or other sensation. For instance, let chocolate ice cream melt on your face, or put lemonade on your morning corn flakes.

Early in the day, while you still have that "morning voice," call a friend, using a foreign accent. See how long you can keep the charade going.

Make music with your kitchen utensils.

Try to run the ink out of your ballpoint pen.

Rather than unceremoniously disposing of your old stuff, dispense with it in a more entertaining manner. Build a funeral pyre for your old socks in the back yard, set them ablaze, then play "Taps" as they go to that big sock drawer in the sky.

Call a friend's answering machine with an important message, planning it so the beep interrupts the most important part of that message. For instance, "Congratulations, Ms. Smith! You've just won 18 million dollars! Please call 555-BEEP!"

Wax your hardwood floors and slide across them in your sweat socks.

Put the end of a roll of bathroom tissue into the toilet and flush. Watch the paper spin off the roll!

Turn a large animal loose in your house.

Turn the volume down on your TV set and make up new dialogue to fit the show.

Ride your bicycle in the house.

PARTIES AT THE OFFICE

Booby trap a coworker's desk. Glue the pencils together. Raise the seat. Lock the drawers. Link all the paper clips in a chain. This is great fun and at the very least will slow productivity to a crawl.

Organize an "Office Olympics." Give prizes for the fastest typist, fastest calculator, fastest phone dialer, etc. And don't forget the "fastest to the parking lot at 5 o'clock!"

Make strange, other-worldly sounds over the intercom. (Works best if you put the phone inside your mouth.)

Swap family pictures to put on your desk. This is especially fulfilling if you have an ugly family.

Kidnap a pet gewgaw from someone's desk. Leave a ransom note. This can lead to hours of high drama.

Organize a monthly office flea market.

Bring a brown bag mini-party to your office. Include a hat, confetti, and a party horn. Be sure to bring extras, as a party of this nature can be contagious.

Keep extra clothes in your office. Each time you come out during the day, wear something different.

Play with office paranoia. Go to another department and measure something, like an empty corner or file cabinet. Nod thoughtfully and say, "There's room." Leave. This will cause an immediate sensation.

Switch nameplates on people's office doors or desks.

Encourage fellow workers to bring their musical instruments to work. Form a "coffee break combo." Within a month or so, you may be giving the Boston Pops a run for their money.

Have some fun with the rumor mill. Circulate an anonymous memo stating, "Get back to me re the new office hours."

If your office floors are tile, and your desk chairs have wheels, you can have an "Office 500" chair race!

When someone is talking on the phone (especially if they are talking to someone important) do everything you can to crack them up.

Call maintenance to report that a black hole is sucking all the light and oxygen out of your office.

Call your department and ask for yourself. See if anyone knows where you are. If they say you're gone for the day, go!

Put a model train layout on your desk.

When anyone knocks on your office door, play a recording of a large, angry, barking dog. Whack your desk with a magazine and shout, "Down, Cujo! Down!" before you open the door.

Adopt a disguise and see if you can fool your coworkers.

Stand outside your building and stare up at the top until you have a whole crowd of fools looking up at nothing.

PARTIES AROUND SCHOOL

Look at your cafeteria food under a microscope. See if it meets government standards for rodent parts.

Form an alternative pep club to cheer for less-popular school activities. For instance, a good debating team cheer would be, "Go, Debaters, Go! Go, Debaters, Go! Kick 'em in the rebuttals! Go, Debaters, Go!" Do the same for the chess team, but do it veeeeery quietly.

Put a phone in your locker. So what if it doesn't work? Act like it does.

Bring your little brother to school as your "science project."

Hold up a "Hi, Mom!" sign at a school assembly.

Fake a coughing fit in the school library.

Wear your pajamas to class, saying that your alarm broke, and you didn't have time to dress.

PARTIES IN CLASS

Try rolling your eyeballs back into your head. Your teacher will be relieved to find out you're not having a seizure.

Try to get the pencil on your desk to move, using only the power of your mind. If this works, get an agent.

Appear to be taking notes, while actually writing a scorching romance novel using your teachers as characters.

Stare at the clock. Try to see the *hour* hand move. While you're at it, see how long you can go without blinking.

See if you can get your shoes and socks off, then back on, without using your hands.

When the teacher turns his back, switch seats with the student in front of you. When he turns his back again, switch back.

Pretend that one side of your body is paralyzed.

Try to wiggle your ears.

Bring an ant to class and let it run around on your desk top.

Using your tongue as a guide, try to draw a picture of the inside of your mouth.

Imagine that, if you press the right spot on your desk, it will rise slowly from the floor, hover, then bank smoothly out the door and fly down the hall, with you in it.

PARTIES ON AN AIRPLANE

Loudly applaud the safety demonstration. Yell, "BRAVO!" and give the stewardess an honest review of her performance.

Make a hand puppet out of an airsick bag.

Gain the confidence of any nervous-looking passenger and tell him that, if he listens carefully, he can hear a wing strut fraying.

Start an airline pillow fight.

Write a note for a passenger on the next flight and leave it in the airline magazine in front of your seat. Tell him about your flight, including a review of the in-flight movie, and what you recommend for dinner.

See how many people you can get into a bathroom.

91

Walk up and down the aisle, asking passengers if they're enjoying the flight, and can you get them anything? If they ask who you are, tell them you own the airline.

Convince your stewardess that you once dated her in high school.

If you are seated next to a stranger, close your eyes and pretend to snore loudly and talk in your sleep.

PARTIES IN A TAXI

Try to convince your driver that you are Al Pacino. This works especially well if the driver is new to this country.

Encourage your driver to radio the dispatcher, saying that he (the driver) has a fare to Rio.

Try to get your driver to sing with you.

Ask your driver if he can break a $500 bill, because that's all you have.

While you're sitting in the back seat, get into a screaming argument with yourself.

Try to convince the driver that it's national "Free Taxi Ride" Day.

Ask the driver why there is a dead possum in the back of his cab.

Tell the driver you're looking for a restaurant that serves roast bat. Assure him that this is a wonderful delicacy, which they eat all the time in Romania.

PARTIES AT THE SUPERMARKET

See if you can buy a single grape. If they're stupid enough not to give it to you for free, they'll spend half the night computing the worth of the little bugger!

Form a large animal out of stuff in the produce section.

Hang around the frozen meat section and give each of the chickens a name as they are selected. See if the customer has the heart to eat a chicken named "Tammy."

PARTIES WHILE STANDING IN LINE

If there is a long line outside a busy restaurant, form alliances. If you're a party of two, ally with another couple, a party of four, and a party of six. That way, if the hostess calls for a party of two, four, six, or eight, you qualify!

Try to get everyone in line to play "Simon Says."

Wheeze on the person in front of you and maybe they'll let you ahead of them.

Offer to be a pen pal to the person behind you.

WHAT A GREAT PARTY SOUNDS like!

Remarks you'd probably hear at a great party in progress, if someone would only turn down the stereo for a moment.

95